World *of* Birds

World

of Birds

Introducing the World of Birds

A visual celebration of the planet's varied and amazing birdlife, *World of Birds* is a unique book in that it distils the 10,500 bird species into 290 full-page images, with these photographs depicting representatives from 90 per cent of the 245 bird families.

The completeness of the collection, and the fact that it contains many rare and sought-after species, lends it strong appeal to keen birdwatchers, while the stunning nature of the images will be appreciated by anyone who has an interest in birds – whether beginner or expert – by showcasing the incredible diversity of birdlife on Earth.

World of Birds contains images covering 220 bird families – from giant flightless ostriches to tiny hummingbirds – in order to depict as wide a diversity as possible of birds worldwide. The pictures have been selected in order to show the varied nature of bird forms and plumages, as well as the range of interesting things they do, including hunting, fighting, feeding, displaying, caring for young, roosting, flocking, migrating, and so on.

Birds utilise virtually every habitat available worldwide, and in some cases the photographs show the birds in the context of their landscape, whether it is Griffon Vultures surveying a Spanish plain, or Dalmatian Pelicans displaying on a lake backed by snow-capped mountains. In other instances images depict a very rare bird or family that may rarely if ever have been included in a book before.

Estimates of the exact number of bird species on Earth vary according to the latest studies, and are changing all the time as we learn more, but for the sake of giving some order to the images *World of Birds* has adopted the IOC's World Bird List as the basis for the listing.

Above all it is hoped that the book will help to raise awareness of the diversity and fragility of birdlife worldwide, and encourage more people to do all that they can to protect it.

Common Ostrich *Struthio camelus*
AFRICA

Greater Rhea *Rhea americana*
SOUTH AMERICA

Southern Brown Kiwi *Apteryx australis*
NEW ZEALAND

Emu *Dromaius novaehollandiae*
AUSTRALIA

Elegant Crested Tinamou *Eudromia elegans*
ARGENTINA

Horned Screamer *Anhima cornuta*
SOUTH AMERICA

Magpie Goose *Anseranas semipalmata*
AUSTRALIA AND NEW GUINEA

Whooper Swan *Cygnus cygnus*
NORTH EURASIA

Snow Goose *Chen caerulescens*

Torrent Duck *Merganetta armata*
SOUTH AMERICA

Common Goldeneye *Bucephala clangula*
NORTHERN HEMISPHERE

Maleo *Macrocephalon maleo*
INDONESIA

Great Curassow *Crax rubra*
SOUTH AMERICA AND CENTRAL AMERICA

Vulturine Guineafowl *Acryllium vulturinum*
AFRICA

Black-fronted Wood-quail *Odontophorus atrifrons*
COLOMBIA

Wild Turkey *Meleagris gallopavo*
NORTH AMERICA

Black Grouse *Lyrurus tetrix*
EURASIA

Greater Sage-Grouse *Centrocercus urophasianus*
NORTH AMERICA

Temminck's Tragopan *Tragopan temminckii*
ASIA

Himalayan Monal *Lophophorus impejanus*
ASIA

Grey Peacock-Pheasant *Polyplectron bicalcaratum*

ASIA

Great Northern Diver or **Common Loon** *Gavia immer*

NORTH AMERICA AND EUROPE

Emperor Penguin *Aptenodytes forsteri*
ANTARCTICA

White-faced Storm Petrel *Pelagodroma marina*
ATLANTIC OCEAN AND AUSTRALASIA

Black-browed Albatross *Thalassarche melanophris*
SOUTHERN OCEANS

European Storm Petrel *Hydrobates pelagicus*
ATLANTIC OCEAN

Black Petrel *Procellaria parkinsoni*
SOUTH PACIFIC

Peruvian Diving Petrel *Pelecanoides garnotii*
OCEANS OFF WESTERN SOUTH AMERICA

Great Crested Grebe *Podiceps cristatus*

EURASIA, AFRICA AND AUSTRALASIA

Andean Flamingo *Phoenicopterus andinus*
SOUTH AMERICA

Red-billed Tropicbird *Phaethon aethereus*
TROPICAL OCEANS WORLDWIDE

Asian Openbill *Anastomus oscitans*
SOUTH ASIA

Roseate Spoonbill   *Platalea ajaja*

Green Heron *Butorides virescens*
NORTH AMERICA AND CENTRAL AMERICA

White Egret *Ardea alba*
WORLDWIDE

Hamerkop *Scopus umbretta*
AFRICA

Shoebill *Balaeniceps rex*
AFRICA

Dalmatian Pelican *Pelecanus crispus*
EURASIA

Magnificent Frigatebird *Fregata magnificens*

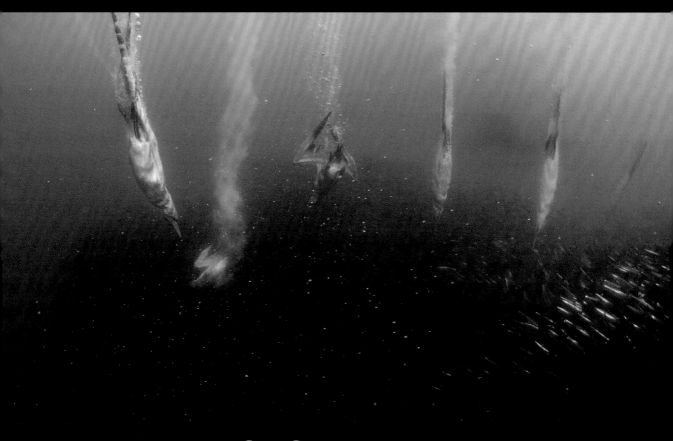

Cape Gannet *Morus capensis*
SOUTHERN AFRICA

Great Cormorant *Phalacrocorax carbo*

EURASIA, AFRICA, AUSTRALASIA AND NORTH AMERICA

Anhinga *Anhinga anhinga*
AMERICAS

King Vulture *Sarcoramphus papa*

SOUTH AMERICA

Secretarybird *Sagittarius serpentarius*
AFRICA

Osprey *Pandion haliaetus*

WORLDWIDE

White-tailed Eagle *Haliaeetus albicilla*
EURASIA

Griffon Vulture *Gyps fulvus*
NORTH AFRICA, SOUTH EUROPE AND SOUTH ASIA

Golden Eagle *Aquila chrysaetos*
EURASIA AND NORTH AMERICA

Black Baza *Aviceda leuphotes*
SOUTH ASIA

Pale Chanting Goshawk *Melierax canorus*
AFRICA

Little Bustard *Tetrax tetrax*
EURASIA

Subdesert Mesite   *Monias benschi*
MADAGASCAR

Red-legged Seriema *Cariama cristata*
SOUTH AMERICA

Kagu *Rhynochetos jubatus*

NEW CALEDONIA

Sunbittern *Eurypyga helias*

CENTRAL AMERICA AND SOUTH AMERICA

African Finfoot *Podica senegalensis*
AFRICA

Ruddy Crake *Laterallus ruber*
SOUTH AMERICA

Water Rail *Rallus aquaticus*
EURASIA

Spotted Crake *Porzana porzana*
EURASIA and AFRICA

Australasian Swamp-hen *Porphyrio melanotus*
AUSTRALIA and NEW ZEALAND

Grey-winged Trumpeter *Psophia crepitans*
SOUTH AMERICA

Red-crowned Crane *Grus japonensis*
EAST ASIA

Limpkin *Amarus guarauna*
AMERICAS

Barred Buttonquail *Turnix suscitator*
ASIA

Eurasian Stone-curlew *Burhinus oedicnemus*
EURASIA

Snowy Sheathbill *Chionis alba*

SOUTHERN SOUTH AMERICA AND ANTARCTICA

Eurasian Oystercatcher *Haematopus ostralegus*
EURASIA

Crab-plover *Dromas ardeola*

COASTAL EAST AFRICA AND SOUTH ASIA

Ibisbill *Ibidorhyncha struthersii*

CENTRAL ASIA

American Avocet *Recurvirostra americana*
NORTH AMERICA AND CENTRAL AMERICA

Northern Lapwing *Vanellus vanellus*
EURASIA AND AFRICA

Piping Plover *Charadrius melodus*
NORTH AMERICA

Egyptian Plover *Pluvianus aegyptius*
AFRICA

Greater Painted-snipe *Rostratula benghalensis*

Comb-crested Jacana *Irediparra gallinacea*
SOUTH ASIA AND AUSTRALIA

Rufous-bellied Seedsnipe *Attagis gayi*
SOUTH AMERICA

Whimbrel *Numenius phaeopus*
WORLDWIDE

Spotted Redshank *Tringa erythropus*
EURASIA

Red Knot *Calidris canutus*
WORLDWIDE

Small Pratincole *Glareola lactea*

SOUTH ASIA

Swallow-tailed Gull *Creagrus furcatus*

GALÁPAGOS AND WESTERN SOUTH AMERICA

Red-legged Kittiwake *Rissa brevirostris*
NORTH PACIFIC

Arctic Tern *Sterna paradisaea*

WORLDWIDE

Black Skimmer *Rhynchops niger*
AMERICAS

Long-tailed Skua or **Long-tailed Jaeger**   *Stercorarius longicaudus*
OCEANS WORLDWIDE

Atlantic Puffin *Fratercula arctica*

NORTH ATLANTIC

Painted Sandgrouse *Pterocles indicus*
INDIAN SUBCONTINENT

Rameron Pigeon *Columba arquatrix*
AFRICA

Turtle Dove *Streptopelia turtur*
EURASIA AND AFRICA

Spinifex Pigeon *Geophaps plumifera*
AUSTRALIA

Hoatzin *Opisthocomus hoazin*
SOUTH AMERICA

Violet Turaco *Musophaga violacea*
AFRICA

Great Spotted Cuckoo *Clamator glandarius*

SOUTH EUROPE, SOUTH-WEST ASIA AND AFRICA

Violet Cuckoo *Chrysococcyx xanthorhynchus*
SOUTH ASIA

Common Cuckoo (chick being fed by adult Eurasian Reed-Warbler) *Cuculus canorus*
EURASIA

Common Barn-Owl *Tyto alba*
WORLDWIDE

Eastern Screech-Owl *Megascops asio*
NORTH AMERICA

Blakiston's Fish-Owl *Bubo blakistoni*
EAST ASIA

Eurasian Pygmy-Owl *Glaucidium passerinum*
EURASIA

Short-eared Owl *Asio flammeus*
EURASIA, NORTH AFRICA AND THE AMERICAS

Sri Lanka Frogmouth   *Batrachostomus moniliger*
SOUTH ASIA

Oilbird *Steatornis caripensis*
SOUTH AMERICA

Great Potoo *Nyctibius grandis*
CENTRAL AMERICA AND SOUTH AMERICA

Nubian Nightjar *Caprimulgus nubicus*
SOUTH-WEST ASIA AND EAST AFRICA

Large-tailed Nightjar *Caprimulgus macrourus*
SOUTH-EAST ASIA AND NORTH AUSTRALIA

Australian Owlet-nightjar *Aegotheles cristatus*
AUSTRALIA

Whiskered Treeswift *Hemiprocne comata*
SOUTH-EAST ASIA

Common Swift *Apus apus*
EURASIA AND AFRICA

Tufted Coquette *Lophornis ornatus*
SOUTH AMERICA

Green Hermit *Phaethornis guy*

CENTRAL AMERICA AND SOUTH AMERICA

Sword-billed Hummingbird *Ensifera ensifera*
SOUTH AMERICA

Ruby-topaz Hummingbird *Chrysolampis mosquitus*
SOUTH AMERICA

Marvellous Spatuletail *Loddigesia mirabilis*

Speckled Mousebird *Colius striatus*

AFRICA

Resplendent Quetzal *Pharomachrus mocinno*
CENTRAL AMERICA

Indian Roller *Coracias benghalensis*
SOUTH ASIA

Scaly Ground Roller *Geobiastes squamiger*
MADAGASCAR

Common Kingfisher *Alcedo atthis*

EURASIA AND NORTH AFRICA

Black-capped Kingfisher *Halcyon pileata*
SOUTH ASIA

Laughing Kookaburra *Dacelo novaeguineae*

AUSTRALIA

Cuban Tody *Todus multicolor*
CUBA

Blue-crowned Motmot *Momotus momota*
CENTRAL AMERICA AND SOUTH AMERICA

Southern Carmine Bee-eater *Merops nubicoides*
SUB-SAHARAN AFRICA

Common Hoopoe *Upupa epops*

EURASIA AND AFRICA

Green Woodhoopoe   *Phoeniculus purpureus*

Southern Ground Hornbill *Bucorvus leadbeateri*

Rhinoceros Hornbill *Buceros rhinoceros*

SOUTH ASIA

Rufous-tailed Jacamar *Galbula ruficauda*

CENTRAL AMERICA AND SOUTH AMERICA

Crescent-chested Puffbird *Malacoptila striata*

Red-headed Barbet *Eubucco bourcierii*

SOUTH AMERICA

Toucan Barbet *Semnornis ramphastinus*
SOUTH AMERICA

Collared Araçari *Pteroglossus torquatus*
CENTRAL AMERICA AND SOUTH AMERICA

Keel-billed Toucan *Ramphastos sulfuratus*
CENTRAL AMERICA AND SOUTH AMERICA

Fire-tufted Barbet *Psilopogon pyrolophus*
SOUTH ASIA

Crested Barbet *Trachyphonus vaillantii*

AFRICA

Lesser Honeyguide *Indicator minor*
AFRICA

White-barred Piculet *Picumnus cirratus*
SOUTH AMERICA

Pileated Woodpecker *Dryocopus pileatus*
NORTH AMERICA

European Green Woodpecker *Picus viridis*
EUROPE AND SOUTH-WEST ASIA

Heart-spotted Woodpecker *Hemicircus canente*
SOUTH ASIA

Southern Caracara *Caracara plancus*

SOUTH AMERICA

Peregrine Falcon *Falco peregrinus*
WORLDWIDE

Kea *Nestor notabilis*
NEW ZEALAND

Major Mitchell's Cockatoo *Lophochroa leadbeateri*
AUSTRALIA

Lilian's Lovebird *Agapornis lilianae*
AFRICA

Red-and-green Macaw *Ara chloropterus*
CENTRAL AMERICA AND SOUTH AMERICA

Yellow-chevroned Parakeet *Brotogeris chiriri*
SOUTH AMERICA

Bronze-winged Parrot *Pionus chalcopterus*
SOUTH AMERICA

Budgerigar *Melopsittacus undulatus*
AUSTRALIA

Ring-necked Parakeet *Psittacula krameri*

ASIA AND AFRICA

Rifleman *Acanthisitta chloris*

NEW ZEALAND

Black-and-yellow Broadbill *Eurylaimus ocromalus*

Velvet Asity *Philepitta castanea*
MADAGASCAR

Malay Banded Pitta *Hydrornis irena*

Garnet Pitta *Erythropitta granatina*

SOUTH ASIA

Rufous Hornero *Furnarius rufus*
SOUTH AMERICA

Strong-billed Woodcreeper *Xiphocolaptes promeropirhynchus*

Red-billed Scythebill *Campylorhamphus trochilirostris*
SOUTH AMERICA

Barred Antshrike *Thamnophilus doliatus*

CENTRAL AMERICA AND SOUTH AMERICA

Ocellated Antbird *Phaenostictus mcleannani*
CENTRAL AMERICA AND NORTH-WEST SOUTH AMERICA

Rufous-breasted Antthrush *Formicarius rufipectus*
CENTRAL AMERICA AND SOUTH AMERICA

Giant Antpitta *Grallaria gigantea*
SOUTH AMERICA

Black-cheeked Gnateater *Conopophaga melanops*
BRAZIL

Millpo Tapaculo *Scytalopus* sp. nov. *millpo*

PERU

Eared Pygmy-Tyrant   *Myiornis auricularis*
SOUTH AMERICA

Pied Water Tyrant *Fluvicola pica*
SOUTH AMERICA

Great Kiskadee *Pitangus sulphuratus*
AMERICAS

Vermilion Flycatcher *Pyrocephalus obscurus*
AMERICAS

Spangled Cotinga *Cotinga cayana*
SOUTH AMERICA

Andean Cock-of-the-rock *Rupicola peruvianus*
SOUTH AMERICA

Golden-collared Manakin *Manacus vitellinus*

PANAMA AND SOUTH AMERICA

Black-tailed Tityra *Tityra cayana*
SOUTH AMERICA

Superb Lyrebird *Menura novaehollandiae*
AUSTRALIA

Satin Bowerbird *Ptilonorhynchus violaceus*
AUSTRALIA

Brown Treecreeper *Climacteris picumnus*

Splendid Fairy-wren *Malurus splendens*
AUSTRALIA

New Holland Honeyeater *Phylidonyris novaehollandiae*
AUSTRALIA

Noisy Friarbird *Philemon corniculatus*
NEW GUINEA AND AUSTRALIA

Spotted Pardalote *Pardalotus punctatus*
AUSTRALIA

Golden-bellied Gerygone *Gerygone sulphurea*
SOUTH-EAST ASIA

Chestnut-crowned Babbler *Pomatostomus ruficeps*

Australian Logrunner *Orthonyx temminckii*
AUSTRALIA

North Island Saddleback *Philesturnus rufusater*
NEW ZEALAND

Stitchbird *Notiomystis cincta*
NEW ZEALAND

Eastern Whipbird *Psophodes olivaceus*
AUSTRALIA

Brown-throated Wattle-eye *Platysteira cyanea*

Bokmakierie *Telophorus zeylonus*

AFRICA

Black-breasted Boatbill *Machaerirhynchus nigripectus*
PAPUA NEW GUINEA

Helmet Vanga   *Euryceros prevostii*
MADAGASCAR

Bornean Bristlehead *Pityriasis gymnocephala*
BORNEO

Ashy Woodswallow *Artamus fuscus*
SOUTH ASIA

Pied Butcherbird *Cracticus nigrogularis*

AUSTRALIA

Common Iora *Aegithina tiphia*
SOUTH ASIA

Black-faced Cuckooshrike *Coracina novaehollandiae*

AUSTRALIA AND PAPUA NEW GUINEA

Whitehead *Mohoua albicilla*
NEW ZEALAND

Varied Sittella *Daphoenositta chrysoptera*

AUSTRALIA

Crested Bellbird *Oreoica gutturalis*
AUSTRALIA

Australian Golden Whistler *Pachycephala pectoralis*

Great Grey Shrike *Lanius excubitor*

EURASIA AND NORTH AFRICA

Blue-headed Vireo *Vireo solitarius*
NORTH AMERICA AND CENTRAL AMERICA

Eurasian Golden Oriole *Oriolus oriolus*
EURASIA AND AFRICA

Bronzed Drongo *Dicrurus aeneus*
SOUTH ASIA

New Zealand Fantail *Rhipidura fuliginosa*
NEW ZEALAND

Indian Paradise Flycatcher *Terpsiphone paradisi*
INDIAN SUBCONTINENT

Steller's Jay *Cyanocitta stelleri*

NORTH AMERICA

Common Raven *Corvus corax*

EURASIA AND NORTH AMERICA

Apostlebird *Struthidea cinerea*
AUSTRALIA

Blue-capped Ifrit *Ifrita kowaldi*
PAPUA NEW GUINEA

Wilson's Bird-of-paradise *Diphyllodes respublica*
NEW GUINEA

Magnificent Bird-of-paradise *Diphyllodes magnificus*

NEW GUINEA

Scarlet Robin *Petroica boodang*
AUSTRALIA

White-necked Rockfowl *Picathartes gymnocephalus*
AFRICA

Drakensberg Rockjumper   *Chaetops aurantius*
AFRICA

Rail-babbler *Eupetes macrocerus*

Bohemian Waxwing *Bombycilla garrulus*

EURASIA AND NORTH AMERICA

Long-tailed Silky-flycatcher *Ptiliogonys caudatus*
CENTRAL AMERICA

Grey Hypocolius *Hypocolius ampelinus*
SOUTH ASIA

Palmchat *Dulus dominicus*
HISPANIOLA

Grey-headed Canary-flycatcher *Culicicapa ceylonensis*
SOUTH ASIA

Great Tit *Parus major*
EURASIA

Tufted Titmouse *Baeolophus bicolor*
NORTH AMERICA

Eurasian Penduline Tit *Remiz pendulinus*
EURASIA

Bearded Tit *Panurus biarmicus*

EURASIA

Eurasian Skylark *Alauda arvensis*

EURASIA

Horned Lark *Eremophila alpestris*

EURASIA, NORTH AFRICA AND THE AMERICAS

Red-whiskered Bulbul   *Pycnonotus jocosus*
SOUTH ASIA

Barn Swallow   *Hirundo rustica*

WORLDWIDE

Sand Martin or **Bank Swallow** *Riparia riparia*
WORLDWIDE

Pygmy Cupwing *Pnoepyga pusilla*
SOUTH ASIA

Long-billed Crombec *Sylvietta rufescens*

AFRICA

Cetti's Warbler   *Cettia cetti*
EURASIA AND NORTH AFRICA

Streaked Scrub Warbler *Scotocerca inquieta*

NORTH AFRICA AND SOUTH-WEST ASIA

Long-tailed Tit *Aegithalos caudatus*
EURASIA

Arctic Warbler *Phylloscopus borealis*
EURASIA AND ALASKA

Great Reed Warbler *Acrocephalus arundinaceus*

EURASIA AND AFRICA

River Warbler *Locustella fluviatilis*
EURASIA AND AFRICA

Black-capped Donacobius   *Donacobius atricapilla*
SOUTH AMERICA

Long-billed Bernieria *Bernieria madagascariensis*
MADAGASCAR

Golden-headed Cisticola *Cisticola exilis*
SOUTH ASIA AND AUSTRALIA

White-browed Scimitar Babbler   *Pomatorhinus schisticeps*

Golden-fronted Fulvetta *Alcippe variegaticeps*
CHINA

Red-tailed Laughingthrush *Trochalopteron milnei*
SOUTH-EAST ASIA

Subalpine Warbler *Sylvia cantillans*
EUROPE AND AFRICA

Black-throated Parrotbill   *Suthora nipalensis*
SOUTH ASIA

Japanese White-eye *Zosterops japonicus*

EAST ASIA

Cape Sugarbird *Promerops cafer*
SOUTH AFRICA

Asian Fairy-bluebird *Irena puella*
SOUTH ASIA

Firecrest *Regulus ignicapillus*
EURASIA AND NORTH AFRICA

Carolina Wren *Thryothorus ludovicianus*

NORTH AMERICA

Black-tailed Gnatcatcher *Polioptila melanura*
NORTH AMERICA

Eurasian Nuthatch *Sitta europaea*
EURASIA

Wallcreeper *Tichodroma muraria*
EURASIA

Short-toed Treecreeper   *Certhia brachydactyla*
EUROPE AND NORTH AFRICA

Northern Mockingbird *Mimus polyglottos*

Superb Starling *Lamprotornis superbus*

AFRICA

Red-billed Oxpecker *Buphagus erythrorynchus*
AFRICA

Varied Thrush *Ixoreus naevius*

Firethroat *Luscinia pectardens*

SOUTH ASIA

European Pied Flycatcher   *Ficedula hypoleuca*

EURASIA AND AFRICA

White-throated Dipper *Cinclus cinclus*
EURASIA

Golden-fronted Leafbird *Chloropsis aurifrons*

Orange-bellied Flowerpecker *Dicaeum trigonostigma*

Greater Double-collared Sunbird *Cinnyris afer*
SOUTH AFRICA

Tree Sparrow *Passer montanus*
EURASIA

Long-tailed Widowbird   *Euplectes progne*
AFRICA

Violet-eared Waxbill *Granatina granatina*
AFRICA

Long-tailed Paradise-whydah *Vidua paradisaea*

Alpine Accentor *Prunella collaris*
EURASIA

Japanese Wagtail *Motacilla grandis*

EAST ASIA

Red-throated Pipit *Anthus cervinus*
EURASIA AND AFRICA

Przevalski's Finch *Urocynchramus pylzowi*
CHINA

Evening Grosbeak *Hesperiphona vespertina*

NORTH AMERICA

Chestnut-bellied Euphonia *Euphonia pectoralis*
SOUTH AMERICA

Chestnut-collared Longspur *Calcarius ornatus*
NORTH AMERICA

Yellowhammer   *Emberiza citrinella*
EURASIA

Chestnut-capped Brushfinch *Arremon brunneinucha*

CENTRAL AMERICA AND SOUTH AMERICA

Western Spindalis *Spindalis zena*
CARIBBEAN

Oriente Warbler *Teretistris fornsi*

CUBA

Subtropical Cacique *Cacicus uropygialis*
SOUTH AMERICA

Cape May Warbler *Setophaga tigrina*

AMERICAS

American Redstart *Setophaga ruticilla*

AMERICAS

Scarlet Tanager *Piranga olivacea*
AMERICAS

Northern Cardinal   *Cardinalis cardinalis*
NORTH AMERICA

Blue-winged Mountain-tanager *Anisognathus somptuosus*
SOUTH AMERICA

Green-headed Tanager *Tangara seledon*

SOUTH AMERICA

Red-legged Honeycreeper *Cyanerpes cyaneus*
CENTRAL AMERICA AND SOUTH AMERICA

Australian Birds In Pictures
Matthew Jones and Duade Paton
ISBN 978 1 92554 634 7

Australian Wildlife On Your Doorstep
Stephanie Jackson
ISBN 978 1 92554 630 9

Chris Humfrey's Awesome Australian Animals
Chris Humfrey
ISBN 978 1 92554 670 5

Field Guide to Birds of North Queensland
Phil Gregory and Jun Matsui
ISBN 978 1 92554 625 5

Parrot Conservation
Rosemary Low
ISBN 978 1 92554 646 0

Slater Field Guide to Australian Birds
Second Edition
Peter Slater, Pat Slater and Raoul Slater
ISBN 978 1 87706 963 5

In the same series as this title:

World of Insects
ISBN 978 1 92554 651 4

World of Mammals
ISBN 978 1 92554 660 6

World of Reptiles
ISBN 978 1 92554 653 8

Australian Wildlife In Pictures
ISBN 978 1 92554 662 0

For details of these books and hundreds of other Natural History titles see
www.newhollandpublishers.com
and follow ReedNewHolland on Facebook and Instagram

First published in 2019 by Reed New Holland Publishers
This paperback edition published in 2022
by Reed New Holland Publishers
Sydney

Level 1, 178 Fox Valley Road, Wahroonga, NSW 2076, Australia

newhollandpublishers.com

A record of this book is held at the National Library of Australia.

ISBN 978 1 92554 663 7

Managing Director: Fiona Schultz
Publisher and Project Editor: Simon Papps
Designer: Andrew Davies
Production Director: Arlene Gippert
Printed in China

10 9 8 7 6 5 4 3 2 1

Keep up with Reed New Holland
and New Holland Publishers
 ReedNewHolland
 @NewHollandPublishers and @ReedNewHolland

Front cover: Resplendent Quetzal *Pharomachrus mocinno* (Trogonidae).
Back cover: Golden-collared Manakin *Manacus vitellinus* (Pipridae).
Page 1: Eye of Northern Harrier *Circus hudsonius* (Accipitridae).
Pages 2–3: Plumage of flamingo (Phoenicopteridae).
Pages 4–5: Plumage of Scarlet Macaw *Ara macao* (Psittacidae).
Pages 6–7: Plumage of Mandarin Duck *Aix galericulata* (Anatidae).
Page 8: Magnificent Hummingbird *Eugenes fulgens* (Trochilidae).